WINDOWS ON WILDLIFE

BY THE SAME AUTHORS

ANDY BEAR
A POLAR CUB GROWS UP
AT THE ZOO

ARE THOSE ANIMALS *REAL?*
HOW MUSEUMS PREPARE
WILDLIFE EXHIBITS

THE CROCODILE AND THE CRANE
SURVIVING IN A CROWDED WORLD

SCALY BABIES
REPTILES GROWING UP

GINNY JOHNSTON AND JUDY CUTCHINS

WINDOWS ON WILDLIFE

MORROW JUNIOR BOOKS · NEW YORK

In the end, we will conserve only what we love. We will love only what we understand. We will understand only what we are taught.

—*Baba Dioum*

PHOTO CREDITS

Permission for the following photographs is gratefully acknowledged: © 1988 Monterey Bay Aquarium, pp. 41, 45; © New York Zoological Society, pp. 26, 27; Everett H. Scott, pp. 23, 24; © 1988 by Sea World, Inc., pp. 18, 21. Reproduced by permission; Joe Sebo, pp. 11, 16; Jerry Wallace, Toledo Zoo, p. 31. All other photographs by Judy Cutchins.

Printed in Singapore by Tien Wah Press (1990).

1 2 3 4 5 6 7 8 9 10

Library of Congress Cataloging-in-Publication Data
Johnston, Ginny.
Windows on wildlife / Ginny Johnston and Judy Cutchins.
p.   cm.
Includes index.
Summary: Illustrates how zoos, wildlife parks, and aquariums
reproduce the wild by designing realistic habitat exhibits for their
plants and animals.
ISBN 0-688-07872-9 — ISBN 0-688-07873-7 (lib. bdg.)
1. Zoos—Juvenile literature.   2. Aquariums, Public—Juvenile
literature.   3. Captive wild animals—Juvenile literature.
[1. Zoos.   2. Aquariums, Public.   3. Captive wild animals.]
I. Cutchins, Judy.   II. Title
QL76.J64   1990
590'.74'4—dc20   89-34487
CIP
AC

ACKNOWLEDGMENTS

The authors wish to thank the following individuals for reviewing chapters of our work and offering their expert comments: Charles Horton, Lead Keeper of the Great Apes, Zoo Atlanta, Atlanta, Georgia; Laura Duckworth-Dennis, Supervisor of Aviculture, Sea World of Orlando, Florida; John Gwynne, Deputy Director for Design, New York Zoological Park, Bronx, New York; David V. Ross, Mammal Keeper, Toledo Zoological Society, Toledo, Ohio; Steven K. Webster, Director of Education, Monterey Bay Aquarium, Monterey, California; and Ron Morris, Curator of Birds, North Carolina Zoological Park, Asheboro, North Carolina.

We also gratefully acknowledge the assistance and encouragement we received from the following: Edward D. Asper, General Curator, Sea World of Orlando, Florida; Jon Coe, President, and Nevin Lash, Associate, Coe, Lee, Robinson, Roesch, Inc., Philadelphia, Pennsylvania; David M. Jenkins, Coordinator, Museum of Natural Sciences, Toledo, Ohio; Elise Gellman Light, Marketing Officer, North Carolina Zoological Park; Terry Maple, Director, and Vaughan Barfield, Executive Assistant to the Director, Zoo Atlanta; Jim Watanabe, Research Biologist, and Roger Phillips, Senior Research Assistant, Monterey Bay Aquarium.

We are indebted to a number of individuals and organizations for their outstanding photographs: Everett H. Scott, Joseph Sebo, Jr., Jerry Wallace, New York Zoological Society, Monterey Bay Aquarium, and Sea World, Inc.

CONTENTS

WHAT ARE
HABITAT EXHIBITS?

The excitement of watching an animal in the wild is unforgettable. What a thrill it is to hear gorillas growl and hoot or watch them care for their young. But few people get a chance to venture into African forests where the great apes live. Many of the world's most fascinating creatures live in habitats too far away or too difficult to visit. However, most people can watch them by visiting a zoo or aquarium.

Until recently, animals in such places were usually caged behind bars, and people walked by to stare at them. The visit held none of the excitement of seeing animals in the wild.

Today, modern zoos, aquariums, and wildlife parks are showing plants and animals in natural-habitat exhibits. These exhibits duplicate a part of an animal's true environment as closely as possible. Since many animals are endangered in their native lands, habitat exhibits may be the only places they can survive.

Building these realistic habitats is not a simple job. It is challenging to build a "river" for hippos or grow a forest indoors. Making rain or snow fall under a roof requires special equipment. Also, before a habitat exhibit can be developed, scientists must spend a great deal of time studying plants, animals, and their natural environment. They watch each species to learn about its way of life and special needs. The scientists then work with exhibit specialists to design a habitat that will be as authentic as they can make it.

Visitors may see more in natural-habitat exhibits than they would see in nature. Windows, for example, allow people to remain warm and dry while watching penguins "fly" under icy water or waddle across snow-covered rocks. Naturalistic exhibits are not only more fun for visitors, but healthier and more comfortable for captive wildlife.

These modern exhibits are much more expensive than cages with bars, but it is worth the money to provide the best possible environment for captive species. The well-being of the plants and animals is the number one goal. Scientists believe that zoo animals live longer and have more babies in naturalistic settings. Raising more young, especially if a species is rare or endangered, will prevent the species from becoming extinct. American zoos no longer take rare animals from the wild for exhibits, so raising these babies is extremely important.

Windows on Wildlife shows readers the amazing ways in which the wild is reproduced in some of the most realistic habitat exhibits in the United States today. These zoos, wildlife parks, and aquariums make every visit an exciting adventure into the real world of wild animals.

FOREST FOR GORILLAS

Slowly the square, white door of the gorilla building slid open. A huge head appeared, and two dark eyes scanned quickly in every direction. It was the gorilla's first look outside in his twenty-seven years at the zoo in Atlanta, Georgia. Captured as a three-year-old in Africa, the male lowland gorilla had lived alone since then in an indoor cage with bars. Now he was about to enter the outdoor area of his new habitat exhibit, the Ford African Rain Forest at Zoo Atlanta. Just outside the gorilla's habitat, the zoo director, exhibit designers, keepers, and news reporters watched anxiously. They wondered what the gorilla's first reaction to the outdoors would be.

The 458-pound gorilla cautiously left the building and moved a few feet away. Hearts beat faster as people watched the powerful ape investigate his new home. He picked up leaves and sniffed them. He felt the grass and looked up at the cloudy sky. The gorilla's old indoor cage of concrete and tile had none of the wonderful smells and sights of the

After twenty-seven years indoors, this western lowland gorilla explores the Ford African Rain Forest exhibit at Zoo Atlanta.

outdoors. A gentle rain began to fall. Confused and startled by the falling drops, the gorilla dashed back inside to safety. Later that day, he ventured out again. Bravely, he ambled farther and investigated every tree and rock on the hillside of the simulated African rain forest. Fallen trees, high grass, and bamboo gave the sloping hillside the appearance of a forest clearing. The curious gorilla seemed to be quite content in his naturalistic home.

Of all the people watching the gorilla that first day, no one was more pleased than his keeper for the past fourteen years. The zookeeper knew the magnificent gorilla would, at last, have a large, interesting place to

The sloping, grass-covered hillside was designed to look like a clearing in an African rain forest.

The gorilla habitats are separated by steep-sided double moats.

live. Although the great ape would still go indoors at night, he would spend each day exploring outside.

In just a few weeks, the lone gorilla had next-door neighbors. The Ford African Rain Forest exhibit was designed for several families of lowland gorillas. The four-and-one-half-acre exhibit is divided so that each family has a separate area. A gorilla family is led by an adult male called a silverback. Since silverbacks in captivity are very protective of their families and their territories, they must be kept apart or they will fight. Moats with steep dirt banks separate the families from each other and from zoo visitors. Each moat is twelve feet deep and fifteen feet across. These moats do not have water in them; instead, thick, soft grass grows at the bottom in case a gorilla tumbles in. The silverbacks can see, smell, and hear each other across the moats, but they cannot get too close.

This realistic habitat design, with families near each other, allows the gorillas to behave much as they would in the wild. In an African forest, gorilla families sometimes meet other families as they search for food. As they approach each other, one male will beat his chest, slap the ground or trees, and run toward the other silverback. This show of strength usually results in one family's moving away, with no actual fighting between the males. In the zoo exhibit, the gorillas cannot reach each other, but they can still display their feelings across the moats. The gorillas, especially the silverbacks, are alert and aware of the activities of the apes living nearby.

At night and in bad weather, the gorillas are kept inside. The holding building for them is hidden behind a wall of giant artificial rocks at the top of the hillside. Each family has its own sliding door into the building. Inside, the families have large, separate, barred cages. During the day, the gorillas eat fruits and vegetables scattered outside by the keepers. Each evening, they receive their main meal of dried food and milk indoors before they sleep.

The gorilla-habitat exhibit looked nothing like a rain forest before builders got started. Twenty-six thousand tons of soil were moved to build a hillside. More than 3,500 trees, shrubs, and flowers were planted to fill in around several hundred trees already growing in the area. Stands of bamboo were planted to make the area look like a sun-filled opening in an African rain forest. The key to success was finding plants that would simulate the look and feel of a rain forest but would survive in Atlanta's cooler, drier climate. For example, southern magnolias that grow in Atlanta were planted because their wide, shiny leaves look very much like the leaves of tropical plants. Some of the exhibit plants must be taken inside a greenhouse for the winter, but most can remain in the exhibit all year round. Rocks and cliffs were made of Gunite, a concrete mixture sprayed over steel wires. The Gunite forms were painted to resemble rocks photographed in Africa. Before the gorillas were released into the exhibit, rock climbers from a nearby university were invited to climb the walls and find any places over which a gorilla might escape.

At Zoo Atlanta, future zookeepers, veterinarians, and scientists will observe gorilla families as part of their training. The Ford African Rain

A young female gorilla, searching for food in the forest clearing, fascinates visitors.

Forest offers close encounters with great apes. Trails wind along outside all four gorilla habitats. At each turn, through the leaves and branches, visitors may spot a gorilla munching bamboo or resting in the sunshine. It is intriguing to watch the delicate and deliberate way apes eat and the gentle way they groom each other. At one place the trail leads through an information building where visitors can learn about gorillas while they watch real ones through a huge window. Gorillas, especially the younger ones, often come close to or even touch the glass. It seems they are curious about people, too.

Watching how gorilla families behave is an important part of the research being done at Zoo Atlanta.

In western Africa, rain forests have been cut and cleared for farms and lumber. As their habitats disappear, gorillas are becoming very rare. Until recently, zoos have not been very successful in raising young gorillas. Fortunately, as more is learned about the needs of the great apes, American zoos are raising larger numbers of healthy youngsters. Since wild gorillas are never captured for American zoos, in a few years, only those born and raised in captivity will be in exhibits.

ICY HOME FOR PENGUINS

t is 9:00 A.M. at Sea World's Penguin Encounter in Orlando, Florida. A perky rockhopper penguin, just eighteen inches tall, bounces from one ice-covered rock to another. Around him dozens of gentoo, chinstrap, and crested macaroni penguins waddle by. Tall king penguins strut about with their flipperlike wings outstretched and orange bills pointed up. An exhibit keeper, dressed in warm, waterproof clothes, carries a bucket filled with fresh fish for the penguins' morning feeding. Each fish was stuffed with vitamins before being placed in the bucket. The keeper holds a small herring in front of an Adélie penguin. The hungry bird gulps the fish headfirst.

Visitors to Penguin Encounter travel on a moving sidewalk in front of windows that are ninety-five feet long. Every day thousands of people look into a simulated Antarctic habitat without disturbing the penguins. Each glass window is three inches thick to hold the tremendous amount of water in the sea pool and to maintain the near-freezing temperatures

Each of the exhibit's two hundred penguins is hand-fed three times a day.

inside the exhibit. The window panels extend below the water so people can watch the penguins swimming in the deep pool. Since the glass is cleaned five times a day, visitors always have a clear view of the penguins.

To duplicate the seasonal changes of sunlight in the Antarctic and to make the penguins feel at home, special lighting is used at Penguin Encounter. When it is summer in North America, it is winter at the South Pole. The sun cannot be seen for several weeks during the Antarctic winter. Imitating this season means keeping the exhibit lights dim from late May until the end of July. The lights are not turned out completely because visitors would not be able to see the penguins. In August, the keepers turn the lights up a little more each morning. By early October, the lights are bright for twenty-four hours a day. This would be like summer at the South Pole, when the sun shines all day and all night.

Simulating the below-zero temperatures of the penguins' natural habitat is not possible at Penguin Encounter, but the birds are kept comfortable by giant air-cooling machines. These machines keep the temperature in the exhibit near freezing all the time. Other machines in the ceiling produce 6,000 pounds of "snow" every twenty-four hours. This finely ground ice falls softly and steadily. Twice a day, keepers shovel it into a smooth layer that melts very slowly. A clear saltwater pool runs the length of the exhibit, and the water is always a chilly 50 degrees. That's about 30 degrees colder than most swimming pools!

A penguin's body is protected by a marvelous feather coat. About seventy shiny, bristly feathers grow from each square inch of skin. These stiff feathers overlap like shingles on a roof. They trap body heat to keep

Through thick glass windows, visitors watch penguins ''fly'' underwater like black-and-white torpedoes.

the penguin warm even during Antarctic blizzards, when the temperature can be 100 degrees below zero. Each day, a penguin uses its curved bill to straighten its feathers. The bird also spreads oil over them from a gland near its tail. The oil and tight, overlapping fit of the feathers keep the skin dry even while the penguin is swimming.

Like those of all birds, a penguin's outer feathers wear out in about a year. These old feathers are shed during the molting season. For one month, while a new set of feathers is growing in, a penguin cannot enter the ocean to find food. Without its warm, waterproof layer, a penguin would quickly die in the icy water. In Antarctica, a penguin may lose nearly half of its body weight while waiting for new feathers. At Penguin Encounter, keepers continue to feed the birds during the molting season.

The Penguin Encounter at Sea World in Orlando, Florida, is not the only Penguin Encounter in the United States. Other exhibits are in California, Ohio, and Texas. Before any were built, teams of scientists studied in Antarctica for six years. They hoped to learn enough about penguins to create suitable habitats for them in America. The scientists watched penguins swim, tumble off rocks into the icy sea, sled across the snow on their bellies, build nests, and raise young. Researchers observed several different species of penguins living close together. They learned that penguins were curious about humans, but not frightened by them.

When the researchers returned to the United States, they worked with a design team to create the first naturalistic exhibit for penguins. It was built at Sea World of San Diego, California, in 1983. Adult penguins were brought to San Diego from Antarctica. They seemed to feel comfortable and behaved very naturally in their indoor home. Some mated and produced eggs.

Since the penguins look so much alike, color-coded bands help researchers and keepers identify each bird.

All the penguins in Penguin Encounters in Ohio, Texas, and Florida were hatched from eggs laid in San Diego. No other adults have been taken from the wild. Although penguins are not endangered species, it is best not to remove animals from their natural habitat or disturb their environment if another way to study them can be found.

Thanks to years of research and careful planning at Penguin Encounters, scientists at last are able to study and raise penguins without traveling thousands of miles to Antarctica. Visitors to the exhibits gain a better understanding of penguins and their unusual, icy habitat.

INDOOR JUNGLE

S tepping inside the huge JungleWorld building at the Bronx Zoo, a visitor enters another world. Not far from the busy streets and bustling crowds of New York City, this simulated Asian rain forest is a jungle adventure. Sounds of birds and insects are everywhere. Splashing waterfalls pour into streams that flow into quiet pools. Tremendous trees, more than fifty feet tall, reach almost out of sight toward skylights in the exhibit ceiling. For the visitor, every sense is awakened because JungleWorld looks, sounds, and even smells like a real rain forest.

This rain forest is completely indoors, so the temperature and amount of moisture in the air can be carefully controlled. Above one of the exhibit's four waterfalls, fog machines spray mist into the air. The moisture forms clouds that drift over the jungle. It is always warm and steamy here, just as it is in a tropical forest. Heating coils hidden beneath the realistic riverbanks at JungleWorld simulate sun-warmed basking

Gharials live in JungleWorld's river. Three separate pools allow the males to set up individual territories.

areas for monitor lizards and crocodilelike gharials.

To add to the rain forest adventure, sounds of insects, birds, and frogs ring out from speakers hidden around the exhibit. These voices were recorded in faraway forests. Live JungleWorld animals answer with calls of their own.

JungleWorld actually includes several rain forest habitats. In a mangrove swamp, playful small-clawed otters grab the tails of proboscis

There are no bars between visitors and this group of rare proboscis monkeys at JungleWorld.

monkeys that perch on low branches; gharials cool themselves in a simulated river; the forest canopy high overhead provides a realistic habitat for troops of monkeys. More than eighty-seven different animal species live under one huge roof at JungleWorld.

In the exhibit, some animals need to be separated from the visitors and from each other. Instead of traditional cages with bars, exhibit builders cleverly used naturalistic barriers. Visitor trails were placed just a little too far from the trees for the proboscis monkeys to leap onto them. Simulated mudbanks are so steep the gharials cannot climb them. Rocky cliffs extend to the ceiling behind spectacular waterfalls. These cliffs provide barriers to separate the three species of monkeys that would not live so close together in the wild. Sleek clouded leopards stretch lazily and watch monkeys play just a few feet away. A clean, almost invisible glass separates the leopards from the monkeys. Predators are not allowed to hunt living prey as they would in the wild, so the leopards must be separated from other animals.

At night most of the animals enter individual holding shelters hidden behind the plants and rockwork of the exhibit. They move readily into their overnight enclosures because this is where they are fed their big meals of the day. Each animal's diet is carefully planned to contain the necessary vitamins and minerals. Once the animals are secured inside their holding pens, keepers observe each individual closely and act quickly if one needs special attention. Every morning while the animals are still in their holding areas, keepers vacuum the floors of the pools and streams. They rake or wash down the jungle floor. Cleanliness is most important in keeping animals healthy.

In the wild, rain forest animals spend much of their time searching for food. To duplicate their natural activities, keepers put some food in the exhibit for the animals to "discover." Fresh leaves, sunflower seeds, and raisins are hidden for the monkeys. This extra food helps keep the leaf eaters from nibbling on the real plants. Crickets are tossed onto the mudbank for the otters. A special "feeding tree" was built for the gibbons. This artificial tree has a secret, bark-covered door in the trunk. Inside, a container is filled with nuts or seeds. Every so often, a device in the tree turns and a few treats fall through pipes and land in openings around the trunk. The quick-learning gibbons search the tree often because they sometimes find a tasty reward. Scientists believe searching for food helps keep the captive animals alert.

Hundreds of exotic ferns, shrubs, and small trees grow throughout the exhibit. But giant rain forest trees could not be brought to JungleWorld. Artificial trees were made with a framework of steel and fiberglass. The "bark" is a layer of hard plastic that was hand carved and painted. Miles

Painted murals realistically show cloud-covered mountains as they look in an Asian rain forest.

of vines wind through the trees of a real rain forest. Gibbons and silvered leaf monkeys use vines to travel quickly through the treetops. Neither of these species spends much time on the ground. But the miles of vines used by the monkeys could not be grown easily in the exhibit. The young, slow-growing vines would constantly be broken by the acrobatic monkeys. So sturdy artificial vines were especially designed for such active climbers.

The vines were made by threading thin steel wires through long nylon ropes. Then the ropes were "slimed." Workers spread gooey rubber all over the ropes. Brown and green colors were mixed into the rubber. When the rubber hardened, the vines were shaped and painted to look

Artists at JungleWorld re-created giant rain forest trees.

as though they were covered with mosses and lichens. Then the vines were twisted and hung all through the tree branches. Some were hung near, but not too near, the trails so visitors can enjoy a close view of long-tailed acrobats in action.

JungleWorld is truly a zoo work of art. It is the first exhibit to combine so many different kinds of animals in one complex indoor habitat. Visitors leave knowing and caring more about the beautiful and valuable rain forest environment where tropical plants and wildlife thrive.

HIPPOQUARIUM

With barely a ripple, the hippo's giant head breaks the surface of the water. A fine mist sprays from the nostrils that open for a breath of air. Tiny ears flick away drops of water. Then, with eyes still closed, the huge head slowly sinks. The hippo is sleeping. About every minute and a half, the 4,000-pound male hippopotamus lifts his head, breathes, and settles back on the river bottom without waking. The water is only six feet deep where the hippo, his mate, and their calf are resting.

It is not unusual for hippos to sleep or doze at the bottom of a river for hours each day. What is unusual is that people can watch these huge mammals in their underwater world. The people are visitors at the Toledo Zoo in Ohio. They see the hippos through large windows in a fascinating exhibit called the Hippoquarium. It is the first exhibit ever built in which zoo designers tried to simulate a quiet African river, the natural habitat of hippos. Few humans have ever been able to observe

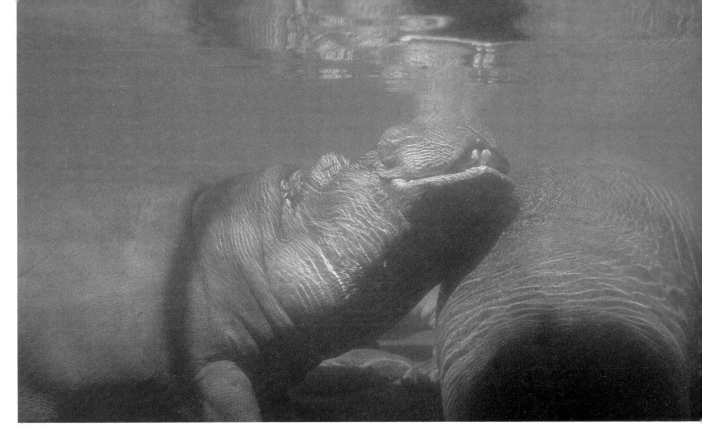

Hippos doze on the bottom of the artificial river just as they would in real rivers of their African homeland.

these wonderful aquatic animals in their muddy and crocodile-filled river homes. At the Hippoquarium, visitors watch through glass panels in a tunnel along one side of the riverlike exhibit. When the hippos are not asleep, they swim and run along the river bottom. Their graceful movements are like a beautiful ballet in slow motion.

Of course, the Hippoquarium is not an exact copy of an African river and riverbank, but the big outdoor exhibit is much more realistic than any previous exhibits for captive hippos. Building this zoo home for hippopotamuses was not easy. The zoo staff wanted to make it comfortable and natural for the animals, as well as exciting for the visitors. The exhibit designers faced some interesting problems.

The first challenge was to create a "river" that would be large enough

Visitors and hippos meet eye to eye at the Hippoquarium in Toledo, Ohio.

to encourage Toledo's two adult hippos to swim around. An enormous hole was dug, and its sides and bottom were coated with concretelike Gunite. Hills and rocks of the same material were shaped into the bottom. Nearly 400,000 gallons of water were pumped in to make the river eight feet deep in places. Several dead logs were anchored to the bottom to make the river more realistic. The river is shallow at one end so the hippos can walk out of the water and lie on the bank.

In Africa, hippos lumber onto the grassy plains at night to graze. Although the exhibit has a riverbank, it does not have a grazing area for the hippos. Instead, they are fed each afternoon inside a large building at one end of the exhibit. Getting the hippos to leave the river and come inside is not a problem because hippos love to eat. The zookeepers walk out on the riverbank and call the animals. In a short time, the giant male, the smaller female, and their calf haul themselves out and head for dinner. Each adult eats twenty-five pounds of plant material and a wheelbarrow load of hay. The calf is still nursing and not yet ready for solid food.

The indoor area is also the winter home for the hippos. It has heated floors and small pools. The animals stay indoors from October to March, when temperatures in Ohio are much colder than those in the hippos' native Africa. Windows on one side of the building allow visitors to look at the hippos when they are indoors.

Perhaps the biggest problem for the Hippoquarium designers was finding a way to keep the river water sparkling clear and clean. This was important for the hippos' health as well as for the visitors' view. Hippos produce many pounds of dung each day. In a real river, the flowing water carries the waste away.

Trees were anchored to the Gunite river bottom for a realistic effect.

While the hippos are indoors, visitors watch as the diver prepares to vacuum the river bottom.

In the Hippoquarium, hippo dung is a problem. The large male, like hippos in the wild, "marks" his territory with dung. He flaps his tail and spreads the dung across the underwater viewing windows. At least once each day, keepers climb above the visitors' tunnel and scrub the windows with long-handled brushes. Large sand filters continuously remove dung from the water. Every hour and a half, all the water is pumped through the filter system. While the water is filtered, chemicals are added that kill harmful bacteria but do not hurt the hippos. A special chemical is put in to cause bits of dirt, hay, and hippo dung to clump together and settle on the bottom. About once a month, a zookeeper in a skin-diving suit swims through the Hippoquarium and vacuums the river bottom. The keeper works while the hippos are indoors feeding. It would be dangerous for someone to be in the hippos' territory with them, because a male protecting his territory or a female defending her calf can be very aggressive. Hippos appear slow and awkward because their stocky legs seem too short for their barrel-shaped bodies. But hippos are very fast swimmers, and they are surprisingly quick on land. Their powerful jaws and large front teeth could seriously injure an intruder.

The Hippoquarium has been a zoo habitat exhibit since 1986. It was the first of its kind in the United States. Now other zoos are building river habitats to provide more lifelike homes for their captive hippos. Each exhibit will be better than the last as zoo designers and zookeepers learn more about the needs and behaviors of these fascinating animals.

The two-ton male hippopotamus lumbers out of the water to rest in the sunshine.

HABITAT FOR TROPICAL BIRDS

One hundred fifty colorful birds with unusual names such as crested barbet, white-fronted bee-eater, and red-faced mousebird sing and call throughout the R. J. Reynolds Forest Aviary. Part of the North Carolina Zoological Park, the aviary is as big as an auditorium. Glass walls and a transparent roof allow sunlight to warm the aviary, creating a giant greenhouse. This indoor woodland simulates the tropical forests of Africa, Asia, and South America. Exotic birds from around the world share this lush enclosure.

Visitors do not watch the birds from behind a window. Instead, they can enter the exhibit and walk among the fascinating birds. A booklet with color pictures helps people identify and name them. With thousands of people visiting the aviary, it might seem that some of the quick-flying birds would accidentally escape through the doorways. Yet this almost never happens. The aviary, which is only open during daylight hours, is always brightly lit by the sun. The entrance and exit hallways are dark.

White African spoonbills and South American scarlet ibises share an artificial stream in the North Carolina Zoo's forest aviary.

Birds will not fly into the dark area. There are two sets of doors in the hallway just in case, but birds rarely leave the lighted aviary.

Inside, a winding pathway takes visitors past trickling streams and rock outcrops that were realistically planned by the zoo's design team. Fig trees from Asia and Africa reach the ceiling to form the forest canopy, or highest level. These tall trees were carefully planted so the soaring birds would have plenty of flying space. Palm, banana, and rubber trees do not grow as tall as the fig trees and so form an understory layer. Canopy and understory trees provide shade and protect the lower levels from the sun's strong rays. Shrubs, vines, and ferns from tropical countries cover the ground. More than 2,000 plants create the multilayered bird habitat. The dense greenery provides hiding places, perches, and nesting materials for fifty-five species of birds.

This green woodhoopoe darts around the understory in search of insects.

The one hundred fifty birds must be observed regularly by the keepers. To make identification of the birds possible, every bird is banded with colored leg bands. No two are alike. Keepers must use binoculars to see the colored bands on tiny lavender finches or scarlet-chested sunbirds. If any bird is not spotted once a month, a serious effort is made to find it. Finding each bird regularly helps the keepers know if one is sick or injured.

The most exciting time of the year in the aviary is nesting season. Each spring, keepers watch for signs of mating and nest building. Bird lovers walking along the curving pathways also search for hidden nests.

When the exhibit was first built, one of the birds gave keepers a special challenge at nesting time. The gray-headed kingfisher from Africa usually digs into mudbanks along creeks and rivers to make its nest. Since the aviary's "mudbanks" are made of wire coated by a layer of rock-hard Gunite, keepers had to give the tunnel nesters a helping hand. They cut a kingfisher-sized hole in the bank and pushed a long plastic tube into it. This duplicated the smooth tunnel made by a kingfisher. It took only a few days for the kingfishers to discover the tunnel and move in to nest. Like most of the aviary birds, they successfully raised young.

Any bird not hatched in the aviary must be introduced to the indoor habitat very carefully. A new arrival is not allowed near the other birds for thirty days in case it has some illness that could spread. During this time, the bird has a complete medical checkup. Before its release, the

The bright red of the scarlet ibis from South America makes this bird one of the first to be spotted by a keeper or an aviary visitor.

newcomer is placed in a cage on the floor of the aviary for a few nights. This gives the stranger time to get used to the sights and sounds of its future home. Three or four flight feathers on each wing are clipped to slow its flying speed. If the bird flies fast at first, it might crash into the clear walls or roof and be seriously hurt. Clipped feathers are shed and replaced by new ones when the bird molts. By that time, the bird is familiar with the aviary and rarely flies into the glass.

Soon after its release, a bird learns where food bowls are placed. Because of the variety of birds, seven different diets are prepared each morning. In addition, some of the nectar feeders drink the sweet juices from orchids and other flowers. Fruit-eating birds gobble up berries as they ripen. Insect eaters catch pests on leaves and flowers. A few birds at the aviary require special diets. For example, the white-fronted bee-eater from Africa eats only insects it catches in the air, so the keepers toss out live insects for the bee-eater to grab.

Since its opening in 1982, the R. J. Reynolds Forest Aviary has

The beautiful gold-fronted leafbird is unafraid of this keeper at feeding time.

The six-sided aviary building has a clear, domed ceiling four stories high.

become a very successful habitat exhibit. Between forty and fifty baby birds are raised each year. Some of the youngsters are sold to other tropical aviaries. This makes it unnecessary to capture birds in their natural habitats for exhibit purposes.

In the aviary, just as in nature, there is much for visitors to discover. If they look quickly and carefully, they will see brilliantly colored birds fly overhead and disappear into the dense forest. The aviary is what a realistic wildlife exhibit should be—a lifelike home for animals and an educational treat for people.

AQUARIUM FOR GIANT KELP

I n the cold, salty water of California's Monterey Bay, there is a most unusual forest. It is a forest of giant kelp. Anchored to rocks on the bay's sandy bottom, the golden seaweed reaches to the surface like Jack's beanstalk. Giant kelp is one of the fastest-growing plants in the world. Each yellow frond can add five or more inches per day. In just a few months, a single frond may grow more than one hundred fifty feet long! The undersea kelp forest is home to an unbelievable variety of sea creatures, such as bat rays, sharks, crabs, otters, starfish, and dozens of kinds of fish. They hide and find food among the kelp fronds. Only scuba divers hardy enough to brave the chilly Pacific Ocean have an opportunity to visit this fascinating marine forest.

Aquarists who study and maintain exhibits at the Monterey Bay Aquarium have found a way to bring some of this underwater wonderland indoors. In the huge aquarium building, they have created dozens of habitat exhibits displaying creatures found in Monterey Bay.

Over two stories high, the towering kelp forest in Monterey Bay Aquarium is the tallest aquarium exhibit in the world.

The largest is the giant kelp forest exhibit. This tank holds 335,000 gallons of seawater—enough to fill 9,000 bathtubs! Because the acrylic windows have to hold back so much water, they must be very strong. Each one is over seven inches thick and weighs 4,400 pounds. With a dozen kelp plants living in the huge tank, it is the only indoor place in the world where visitors can see the tangled, swaying fronds of living giant kelp.

Hundreds of fish swim among the kelp fronds while starfish, anemones, and sea urchins hold tightly to the tank's artificial rockwork. Powerful pumps bring 2,000 gallons of water a minute into the aquarium from Monterey Bay. The pipes for incoming water reach far into the bay and bring in water from sixty feet below the surface. Water

Looking through the aquarium windows, visitors get a diver's-eye view without getting wet.

brought in from this cold depth keeps the temperature in the tank between 50 and 55 degrees year round.

The natural seawater is murky and cloudy because it is filled with microscopic living and nonliving particles. Tiny shrimplike creatures, baby starfish, crabs, and seaweed spores are pumped in. Some of these settle on the rocky ledges and grow up in the tank. Others are eaten by the fish, larger starfish, or sea anemones. The dissolved nutrients in the seawater are essential for healthy growth of all living things in the tank. But the ocean water is too cloudy to allow visitors to get a good view. So at three o'clock each morning, a special keeper presses buttons that cause the incoming seawater to follow a different route. Instead of going directly into the kelp forest tank, the water passes through large sand filters. By 10:00 A.M., when the aquarium opens, the water is clear enough for good viewing. Every evening at closing time, the system is reversed, and the cloudy, nutrient-rich seawater is once again pumped straight into the kelp tank.

Giant kelp has never been kept alive in tanks for long because it needs the waves and currents of the ocean. Without moving water, the flattened blades of giant kelp cannot absorb enough nutrients for the seaweed to survive. Kelp also must have plenty of sunlight.

The designers of Monterey Bay Aquarium solved both problems. The huge tank is open at the top to allow sunlight to reach the seaweed. Additional lights placed above the surface are used when the aquarium's walls shade the kelp. The problem of making the water move was solved by the invention of a surge machine. A huge plunger on top of the aquarium pushes down into the water every thirty seconds. Each powerful plunge creates a water surge equal to a one-foot wave in the ocean. Visitors cannot see the plunger because it is hidden behind the tank's rockwork. What they do see through giant windows is a kelp forest swaying gently back and forth, much as it does in Monterey Bay.

Twice each day the surge machine is turned off so a diver can enter the tank and feed the hundreds of fish. The diver carries a plastic bag filled with fifteen pounds of fresh fish, shrimp, and squid. Eagerly, the fish take food right from the diver's hands as he or she moves to the different levels of the tank.

Normally, giant kelp plants live only three or four years. When one in the tank dies, divers go into the bay to get a replacement. The tall, lacy seaweed does not have roots. Instead, it has strong, weblike holdfasts that cling to rocks. A diver pries the kelp's holdfasts loose with a crowbar. Then, back in the exhibit tank, the kelp is anchored to artificial

Divers feed the aquarium fish, trim the fast-growing kelp, and clean the huge windows.

Researchers dive in Monterey Bay to study the growth rate of giant kelp in its natural environment.

rocks, using strong rubber cords. After a few weeks the fast-growing kelp takes hold in its new home.

Research shows that the kelp and animals in the aquarium live and grow very much as they do in the ocean. Through this realistic and beautifully designed habitat exhibit, visitors get a rare look at the magnificent world below the ocean's surface.

LIFE IN THE WILD VERSUS LIFE IN CAPTIVITY

Natural-habitat exhibits are exciting places and fun to visit. They are realistic homes away from home for plants and animals, and they let people peek into those fascinating worlds.

But artificial habitats are not perfect. Designers know that nature is far too complex to be duplicated. Some parts of a naturalistic exhibit are very different from the wild. In captivity, for example, plants and animals are tended by keepers specializing in their care. Many exhibit animals are taken indoors at night and during bad weather. Protected from their enemies, zoo animals receive expert medical attention and perfectly balanced meals. Even with such care, zookeepers may not meet every need of a captive species because all of its needs are not yet understood.

Living freely in its own natural environment is, of course, ideal for any living thing. But many wildlife habitats are disappearing. In much of the world people have moved in, cleared the land, and even killed the animals for their own needs. Thousands of plant and animal species are nearing extinction. As conservationists fight to save natural areas, zoos and aquariums have taken on the challenge of protecting some of the rare and endangered species. Natural-habitat exhibits provide safe and healthy places for plants and animals while helping visitors understand their world a little better.

GLOSSARY

aquarist—one who takes care of water-living animals and plants in an aquarium.

aviary—an enclosure for keeping birds.

canopy—the umbrellalike layer of a forest formed by the tops of the tallest trees.

conservationist—a person concerned about preserving living things and their environments.

endangered—threatened with extinction.

environment—the combination of air, food, water, space, and other resources used by a plant or animal.

extinct species—an animal or plant species that has died out.

frond—the leaflike structure of a seaweed.

Gunite—a concrete mixture sprayed over steel wires to create artificial settings.

habitat—the home of a plant or animal.

habitat exhibit—a naturalistic display for plants or animals designed to duplicate their real-life home.

moat—a deep, wide ditch used as a barrier to enclose animals in habitat exhibits.

molt—to shed outer feathers while growing new ones.

nutrient—substance used for growth and development.

rain forest—a type of forest rich in plant and animal life that is kept green all year round by high rainfall and mild temperatures.

simulate—to copy or duplicate as closely as possible.

understory—the level of a forest formed by the tops of trees that do not reach the canopy.

INDEX

Illustrations are indicated by *italics*.

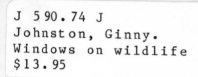